C0-ATF-385

Design for the Ballet

by

CYRIL W. BEAUMONT

The Special Winter Number of The Studio, 1937
Edited by C. G. Holme

LONDON: THE STUDIO LTD., 44, LEICESTER SQUARE, W.C. 2
NEW YORK: THE STUDIO PUBLICATIONS INC., 381 FOURTH AVE.

ACKNOWLEDGMENTS

The Author desires to express his acknowledgments to the artists who have kindly allowed their designs to be reproduced and in particular to those who have lent original drawings for reproduction.

The Author also wishes to record his grateful appreciation of courtesies afforded him by M. Rolf de Maré and Dr. Pierre Tugal, respectively Founder-Director and Keeper of Les Archives Internationales de la Danse, Paris ; M. J-G. Prod'homme, Keeper of the Musée de l'Opéra, Paris ; Messrs. Tooth's Galleries, London—the designs by A. Benois being derived from their recent exhibition of that artist's work ; Col. W. de Basil ; M. René Blum ; M. Adolph Bolm ; Miss Derra de Moroda ; Anton Dolin, Esq. ; M. Poul Eltorp ; Dr. Paolo Fabbri ; M. Gyula Harangozó ; the Society for Cultural Relations with Foreign Countries, Moscow ; Geoffrey Keynes, Esq. ; Albert W. King, Esq. ; Lincoln Kerstein, Esq. ; Serge Leslie, Esq. ; Miss Catherine Littlefield ; Miss Ruth Page ; Robert E. Jones, Esq. ; *The Dance* Magazine, New York ; Dr. Walter Toscanini ; and John V. Trevor, Esq., in connection with the loan and assembling of material.

Reg. U.S. Pat. Off.

Printed and Engraved in Great Britain by Herbert Reiach Ltd., 43, Belvedere Road, London, S.E.1

1928
Bea

Contents

INTRODUCTION 7

Scenic design and costume in the Imperial Russian Ballet. New forces in stage decoration in the 1890's. The influence of Mamontov. Wolkonsky and Teliakovsky. Diaghilev in Paris. 1906-19; the work of Benois, Bakst, Roehrich and the Russians. 1917 and the French modernists.

The Ballets Suédois of Rolf de Maré; the experiments of Léger, Andrée Parr and Picabia. Productions of the Ballets Russes de Col. de Basil and the Ballets de Monte Carlo of René Blum. The Soviet Ballet. The Paris Opera ballet. The Ballet Jooss. Denmark, Czechoslovakia, Italy. The U.S.A.: Adolph Bolm, Michel Fokine, etc.; the American Ballet. English designers. The Camargo Society. The Vic-Wells Ballet. The Markova-Dolin Company.

The stage setting in relation to Ballet. The significance of costume and considerations governing costume design.

The possibilities of Ballet design to-day.

INDEX TO THE ILLUSTRATIONS

(An asterisk by a page reference indicates a colour plate)

Designers

ABELL, Kjeld, 150
AGNEW, Eric, 149
ANDREU, Mariano, 128, 130, 131*
ANNENKOV, Georges, 64, 65
AUD, Jon, 79

BAKST, Léon, 28, 29
BASSADOUA, 100
BAUCHANT, André, 51
BEATON, Cecil, 110, 113
BEAUMONT, Comte Etienne de, 82
BELL, Vanessa, 70
BENOIS, Alexandre, 52, 53*, 55
BENOIS, Nadia, 71*, 99
BENOIS, Nicholas, 63, 120
BERAIN, Jean, 49
BERARD, Christian, 95, 103, 129
BERNERS, Lord, 143
BILINSKY, B., 148
BOUCHENE, Dmitri, 141
BROGGI, Achille, 77

CARAMBA, 147
CASSANDRE, A., 112
CHANEL, 43
CHANEY, Stewart, 51
CHAPPELL, William, 57, 70, 87, 101, 104, 140
CHIRICO, Giorgio de, 39*, 58
COLIN, Paul, 25*, 78, 145
COROT, J.-B., 123

DE BRY, Theodore, 106
DERAIN, André, 103, 119, 127
DMITRIEV, V. V., 68, 124
DOBUZHINSKY, Mitislav, 73, 86, 88, 89*, 105, 112, 122
DOLTON, Phyllis, 50, 109
DUFY, Raoul, 102

FEDOROVICH, Sophie, 80, 100, 118, 144
FEDOROVSKY, F. F., 92, 93
FFOULKES-JONES, Marjorye, 138
FILOMARINO, Prince Mario Cito, 74, 134
FULOP, Zoltan, 75, 85, 121, 146, 152

GABO, 48
GONCHAROVA, Natalia, 18, 32, 33*, 35, 42, 66
GOUGH, Philip, 59
GRIS, Juan, 46
GUYS, Constantin, 82

HALICKA, Alice, 137
HALLSTROEM, Gunnar, 20
HECKROTH, Hein, 17, 61, 116
HELLE, André, 22
HOWARD, Andrée, 94
HUGO, Jean, 31

JOHANNSEN, Svend, 79, 150
JONES, Robert Edmond, 17, 21

KHODASEVICH, V. M., 60, 98
KIRSTA, George, 136
KROCHT, Per, 47

LAGUT, Irène, 39*
LAPRADE, Pierre, 23
LARIONOV, Michel, 19, 30, 32, 33*, 66
LARTHE, M., 102
LAURENCIN, Marie, 43
LAURENS, Henri, 43
LEGER, Fernand, 36, 37, 114
LOURIE, Eugène, 81

MARK, Tivadar, 151
MARTIN, Charles, 58
MARTIN, Keith, 106
MASSON, André, 81

MATRUNIN, B. A., 84
MENINSKY, Bernard, 115
MIRO, Joan, 67
MOTLEY, 46, 91
MOUVEAU, 20
MURPHY, Gerald, 41

NERMAN, Einar, 24
NOGUCHI, Isamo, 139

OLAH, Gusztav, 69, 75, 85, 107*, 146, 152
OLGYAY, Aladár, 151

PAGE, Ruth, 139
PARR, Andrée, 25*, 27
PERDRIAT, Hélène, 38
PETRITSKY, Anatol, 45
PEVSNER, 48
PICABIA, Francis, 44
PICASSO, Pablo, 94
PINTO, Angelo, 138, 142
POLUNIN, Vladimir, 82

RABINOVICH, Isaac, 125
RAVERAT, Gwendolen, 71*
REMISOV, Nicholas, 49, 139
ROTA, Titina, 76, 77
ROVESCALLI, Antonio, 147

SANTONI, G. B., 147
SHARAFF, Irene, 133
SHERINGHAM, George, 83
STEVENSON, Hugh, 95, 96, 97, 111, 135, 148
SUDEIKINE, Sergey, 56
SZUNYOGH-TUDOS, Klára, 151

TCHELITCHEV, Pavel, 67, 117
TERECHKOVICH, Constantin, 81

VELLANI-MARCHI, M., 76

WHISTLER, Rex, 126

ZAMPINI, M. 123

Ballets

ANNA ANNA, 150
APOLLON MUSAGETE, 51
APPARITIONS, 113
ARLEQUINADE, 86
AUBADE, 112
AUCASSIN AND NICOLETTE, 46
AZ ONZO ORIAS, 75

BAISER DE LA FEE, LE, 100, 118, 137
BALLADE, 17
BAR AUX FOLIES BERGERE, 57
BARN DANCE, 142
BEACH, 102
BEAU DANUBE, LE, 82
BELKIS, QUEEN OF SHEBA, 63
BELLE AU BOIS DORMANT, LA, 73, 125
BERCEUSE, 77
BICHES, LES, 43
BIEN AIMEE, LA, 52, 136
BIRDS, THE, 76, 123
BIRTHDAY OF THE INFANTA, THE, 21
BOITE A JOUJOUX, 22
BOLERO, 79
BOUTIQUE FANTASQUE, LA, 127

CAPRIOL SUITE, 57
CARD PARTY, THE, 133
CASSE-NOISETTE, 104, 122
CHATTE, LA, 48
CHOREARTIUM, 81
CHOUT, 30
COMEDIENS JALOUX, LES, 64
CONCURRENCE, LA, 127
CONTES RUSSES, 19
COPPELIA, 112
COQ D'OR, LE, 18, 53*
CORSAIRE, LE, 45
COTILLON, 95
CREATION DU MONDE, LA, 37
CSARDAJALENT, 121
CSONGOR ES TUNDE, 146

DANSES VILLAGEOISES, 74
DARK ELEGIES, 71*
DAVID, 115
DAVID TRIOMPHANT, 113
DEATH IN ADAGIO, 115
DESCENT OF HEBE, THE, 99
DIABLE DANS LE BEFFROI, LE, 47
DON JUAN, 130, 131*
DREAMS, 103
DWARF GRENADIER, THE, 105

EL GRECO, 20
ELEMENTS, LES, 141
EPREUVE D'AMOUR, L', 119
ESMERALDA, 60

FABOL FARAGOTT KIRALYFI, 75
FINANCES, 145
FLAMES OF PARIS, THE, 68
FOIRE DE SOROCHINSK, LA, 33*
FOUNTAIN OF BAKHCHISARAY, THE, 98
FUN IN A TOY SHOP, 59

GALLANT ASSEMBLY, 148
GISELLE, 101
GODS GO A-BEGGING, THE, 95
GREEN TABLE, THE, 61

HARLEQUIN FOR PRESIDENT, 106
HAUNTED BALLROOM, THE, 91
HIGH YELLOW, 70
HOLY TORCH, THE, 121
HOMME ET LA MACHINE, L', 78
HOMME ET SON DESIR, L', 25*, 27
HUNGARIAN FANTASY, 85

ICARE, 102
IMPRESSIONS OF A BIG CITY, 116
INN SCENE, 121

JAR, THE (Vic-Wells Ballet), 87
JARDIN AUX LILAS, LE, 111
JARRE, LA (Ballets Suédois), 39*, 58
JEUX D'ENFANTS, 67
JOB, 71*
JOSZI THE WISE, 146
JOTA ARAGONESA, 128

KALEVALA, 97
KURUC FAIRY TALE, 69, 107*

LAC DES CYGNES, LE, 135
LITTLE JOHNNY IN TOP BOOTS, 152
LORD OF BURLEIGH, THE, 83
LOST ILLUSIONS, 124
LOVE OF THE THREE POMEGRANATES, THE, 120
LUMAWIG, 134
LYSISTRATA, 57

MAGYAR ABRANDOK, 85
MARCHAND D'OISEAUX, 38
MARIES DE LA TOUR EIFFEL, LES, 31, 39*
MASQUE OF THE RED DEATH, THE, 59
MASQUES, LES, 80
MEPHISTO VALSE, 100

MERMAID, 94
MOUVEMENT, LE, 78
MOZART TRIO, 149
MOZARTIANA, 103

NIGHTINGALE AND THE ROSE, THE, 50, 109
NOCES, 42
NOCES DE PSYCHE ET L'AMOUR, LES, 52, 53*
NOCTURNE, 144
NURSERY SUITE, THE, 104

ODE, 67
OFFERLUNDEN, 20
OISEAU DE FEU, L', 35
OLD MILAN, 147
ORCHESTRE EN LIBERTE, L', 49
ORPHEUS, 117

PAN, 83
PATINEURS, LES, 140
PAVILLON, LE, 110
PERHAPS TOMORROW !, 151
PLANETS, THE, 96
POCAHONTAS, 106
PRESAGES, LES, 81
PRINCE CARVED FROM WOOD, THE, 75
PRINCE IGOR, 73, 92, 93
PRINCESSE CYGNE, LA, 55, 148

RAKE'S PROGRESS, THE, 126
RAYMONDA, 88, 89*
RED POPPY, THE, 62
RELACHE, 44
RENARD, 32, 33*
RUGBY, 145
RUSTRE IMPRUDENT, LE, 58

SADKO, 55, 56
SAILORS' LOVE, 116
SCULPTURE NEGRE, 25*
SCUOLA DI BALLO, 82
SELFISH GIANT, THE, 75
SIEBA, 147
SKATING RINK, 36
SLEEPING PRINCESS, THE, 28, 29
SUR LE BORYSTHENE, 66
SYLPHIDES, LES, 105, 123
SYMPHONIE FANTASTIQUE, 129
SZENT FAKLYA, 121

TENTATIONS DE LA BERGERE, LES, 46
TERMINAL, 138
THREE-CORNERED HAT, THE, 74, 94
THREE FAT MEN, THE, 84
TOMBEAU DE COUPERIN, LE, 23
TRAGEDY OF THE CELLO, THE, 49
TRAIN BLEU, LE, 43, 79
TRICORNE, LE, 74, 94
TYL EULENSPIEGEL, 17

VALENTINE'S EVE, 118
VARIATIONS, 65
VEUVE DANS LE MIROIR, LA, 150
VIERGES FOLLES, LES, 24

WEDDING BOUQUET, THE, 143
WITHIN THE QUOTA, 41

Ballet Companies, Composers, Choreographers, etc.

Adam, Adolphe, 45, 101
Adami, G., 147
Allatini, Eric, 130, 131
American Ballet Company, 51, 103, 117, 133, 137
Antheil, George, 103
Asafiev, B. V., 68, 98, 124
Ashton, Frederick, 57, 70, 80, 83, 100, 113, 118, 140, 143, 144
Atterberg, Kurt, 24
Auric, Georges, 127

J. S. Bach., 52, 53
Balanchine, George, 48, 51, 95, 103, 112, 117, 127, 133, 137
Ballet Caravan, The, 106
Ballet Ida Rubinstein, 52, 53, 55
Ballet Rambert, 57, 71, 80, 94, 96, 99, 100, 111, 118
Ballets de Monte Carlo (de René Blum), 104, 112, 119, 123, 128, 130, 131, 141
Ballets Jooss, 17, 61, 116
Ballets Russes de Col. W. de Basil, 35, 110, 127, 129
Ballets Russes de Monte Carlo, 67, 81, 82, 95, 102, 127
Ballets Suédois (de Rolf de Maré), 20, 22, 23, 24, 25, 27, 31, 36, 37, 38, 39, 41, 44, 58
Balzac, H. de, 124
Baratov, 92
Bartók, Béla, 75
Basil, Col. W. de : see Ballets Russes
Beecham, Sir Thomas, 95
Begitchev, V. P., 135
Benois, Alexandre, 52, 136
Berlioz, Hector, 129
Berners, Lord, 143
Bielsky, V., 18
Bizet, Georges, 67
Bloch, Ernest, 99
Blum, René : see Ballets de Monte Carlo
Boccherini, 82
Bolm, Adolph, 21, 49
Borlin, Jean, 20, 22, 23, 24, 25, 27, 31, 36, 37, 38, 39, 41, 44, 58
Borodine, 92, 110
Brada, Rezsö, 69, 75, 107, 121
Bradley, Buddy, 70
Brahms, 81
Brecht, Berl, 150

Camargo Society, 70, 71, 83
Canudo, Riciotto, 36
Carpenter, John Alden, 21
Carter, Elliott, 106
Casella, Alfredo, 39, 58, 87
Cendrars, Blaise, 37
Chabrier, Emmanuel, 57, 95
Chausson, 111
Chicago Opera Association, 21
Chopin, 105, 123
Christensen, B., 150
Christensen, Lew, 106
Cieplinsky, Jan, 75, 85, 146
Claudel, Paul, 25, 27
Clementis, E., 152
Cocteau, Jean, 31, 39, 43, 79
Cohen, F. A., 61
Colman, 17
Coralli, Jean, 101

Debussy, Claude, 22, 114
Delibes, Leo, 112
Delius, Frederick, 144
Derain, André, 103, 119
Diaghilev Ballet Company, 17, 18, 19, 28, 29, 30, 32, 33, 35, 42, 43, 46, 48, 51, 67, 94
Dmitriev, V. V., 68
Dohnányi, Ernst von, 121
Dolin, Anton, 50, 109
Drigo, Richard, 86

Elgar, Sir Edward, 104

Falla, Manuel de, 74, 94
Field, Marjorie, 59
Fokine, Michel, 18, 35, 105, 119, 120, 123, 128, 130, 131, 141
Fornaroli, Cia, 76, 77
Françaix, Jean, 102

Galafres, Elsa von, 121
Gautier, Théophile, 101
Geltser, 135

Glazunov, A., 88
Glière, R. M., 62
Glinka, 128
Gluck, 117, 130, 131
Gordon, Gavin, 126
Grétry, 74
Guastalla, C., 63, 76
Guerra, Nicholas, 47
Guion, D., 142

Handel, 95
Haquinius, Algot, 20
Harangozó, Gyula, 121, 151, 152
Harsányi, Zsolt, 69, 107
Holbrook, Joseph, 46
Holst, Gustav, 96
Honegger, Arthur, 36
Howard, Andrée, 94
Hubay, Jenö, 75, 121
Hughes, Spike, 70

Inghelbrecht, D. E., 20
Italian Chamber Ballet, 76, 77
Ivanov, Leo Ivanovich, 135

Jacobson, Maurice, 115
Jooss, Kurt, 17, 61, 116
Juhász, I., 151

Kenessey, J., 151, 152
Kerdyk, R., 102
Keynes, Geoffrey, 71
Kingsley, Herbert, 138
Kochno, Boris (see also Sobeka), 67
Kodály, Zoltán, 69, 107
Kósa, G., 146
Kurilko, M. T., 62

Lambert, Constant, 113
Lander, Harold, 79, 150
Lányi, Viktor, 121
Larionov, Michel, 30
Leeder, Sigurd, 116
Lester, Keith, 115
Liadov, 19
Lichine, David, 110
Lifar, Serge, 32, 66, 102, 114
Liszt, 52, 85, 100, 113, 136
Lithuanian Ballet, 73, 86, 88, 105
Littlefield, Catherine, 138, 142
Lopukhov, F. V., 62
Loring, Eugene, 106
Lualdi, A., 134
Lualdi, M., 134

Mahler, 71
Maliev, 133
Manzotti, Luigi, 147
Maré, Rolf de: see Ballets Suédois
Marenco, R., 147
Markova-Dolin Ballet, 46, 115, 136
Márkus, L., 85, 146
Massine, L., 19, 63, 67, 81, 82, 94, 102, 127, 129, 147
Maudrick, Lizzie, 74
Mazilier, 45
Mendelssohn, 83
Meyerbeer, 140
Milhaud, Darius, 25, 27, 37, 43, 79
Millos, Aurel, 69, 107
Mohacsi, E., 146
Moiseyev, I. A., 84
Molière, J.-B., 64
Monteclair, 46
Mozart, 103, 119, 141
Murphy, Gerald, 41
Mussorgsky, Modeste, 33, 114

Nabokov, N., 67
Nemchinova-Dolin Ballet, 50
Nerman, Einar, 24
Nijinska, Bronislava, 33, 43, 46, 52, 53, 55, 64, 65, 100, 136, 148
Nijinska's Théâtre de la Danse, 64, 65, 148
Nijinsky, Vaslav, 17
Nuitter, Charles, 112

Olecha, I., 84
Opéra et Ballet Privés de Paris, 33
Oransky, V. A., 84

Pashkov, Lydia, 88
Perrot, Jules, 60
Petipa, Marius, 28, 73, 88, 125, 135
Philadelphia Ballet Company, 138, 142
Picabia, Francis, 44
Pick-Mangiagalli, Riccardo, 77
Pirandello, Luigi, 39, 58, 87
Porter, Cole, 41
Poulenc, Francis, 43, 80, 112
Powell, J., 142
Pratesi, 74
Preston, H., 105
Prokofiev, Sergey S., 30, 57, 66
Pugni, Cesare, 60

Ralov, Börge, 150
Rambert, Marie: see Ballet Rambert
Ravel, Maurice, 23, 79, 94, 118
Respighi, Ottorino, 63, 76, 123
Rieti, Vittorio, 114
Rimsky-Korsakov, N., 18, 55, 56, 148
Romanov, Boris, 104, 134
Rossini, 127
Royal Hungarian State Ballet, 69, 75, 85, 107, 121, 146, 152
Rubinstein, Ida: see Ballet Ida Rubinstein

Saint-Georges, V. de, 45, 101
Saint-Léon, Arthur, 112
Salaman, Susan, 94
Satie, Erik, 44
Sauguet, Henri, 48
Scarlatti, 106, 115
Schubert, 52, 136
Scott, Cyril, 59
Sierra, Martinez, 94
Simson, H. Fraser, 50
Six, The, 31, 39
Slavinsky, Thaddeus, 30
Sobeka (*nom de plume* of Boris Kochno), 48
Sonzogno, G. C., 120
Soviet State Ballet, 45, 60, 62, 68, 84, 98, 124, 125
Staats, Leo, 58
Strauss, Johann, 82
Strauss, Richard, 17
Stravinsky, Igor, 32, 33, 35, 42, 51, 100, 118, 133, 137
Szyfer, J. E., 102

Tailleferre, Germaine, 38
Tansman, Alexander, 49, 116
Tartini, 148
Tchaikovsky, P. I., 28, 73, 81, 104, 125, 135
Tod, Quentin, 59
Toye, Geoffrey, 91
Toye, Wendy, 46
Tudor, Antony, 57, 71, 96, 97, 99, 111, 148

Valois, Ninette de, 57, 71, 87, 91, 95, 104, 126
Vanda, Poppaea, 115
Vic-Wells Ballet, 87, 91, 95, 101, 104, 113, 118, 122, 126, 135, 140, 143, 144
Vittadini, F., 147
Volkov, N. D., 68, 98
Vynonen, V. I., 68

Wallmann, Margarete, 123
Warlock, Peter, 57
Weill, Kurt, 150
Weiner, L., 146
Wilde, Oscar, 21, 75
Williams, Vaughan, 71

Zakharov, R. V., 98
Zverev, Nicholas, 105, 112

Introduction

This collection of designs for settings and costumes for Ballet is intended to afford a pictorial survey of the work accomplished in that field during the last fifteen years. This survey does not pretend to be exhaustive, but it is representative of the development of stage decoration in relation to Ballet. The period under review begins soon after the second decade of the Diaghilev Company. I have deliberately omitted reference to the earlier phase of Diaghilev's activity, since this has been fully covered in other works.

The first realisation of a ballet as an artistic whole, in which scenery, costume, music, and choreography are combined in harmony with one another and with the theme is due to Michel Fokine, and may be said to date with the production at St. Petersburg, on November 25th, 1907, of his ballet, *Le Pavillon d'Armide*.

Previous to Fokine the Imperial Russian Ballet had been ruled by Marius Petipa, whose reign endured for fifty years. In the ballet of those days everyone worked independently—choreographer, composer, and scene-designer—and when the whole was assembled the result frequently left a great deal to be desired.

The scene-designer had a competent knowledge of historical ornament and the style of architecture characteristic of different epochs, but his work was dull and mechanical, devoid of style-atmosphere and interest. The designer's chief concern was to achieve a sense of space and magnificence, and to exploit the laws of perspective to achieve impressive effects of distance.

The costumes presented a strange contrast in that those of the supers were often historically correct according to the period of the ballet, while the dancers, from *corps de ballet* to *danseuse étoile*, wore the ballet-skirt, pink tights, and satin shoes of tradition. Period and nationality were suggested by decorative motifs applied to the ballet-skirt. Another curious convention was the dancer's *coiffure*, which followed the fashion of the moment, whatever the character represented, and was often decorated with a diamond crescent or tiara.

These conditions may be said to have been in force in the ballet companies of all European countries in the second half of the 19th century.

Let us leave the Ballet for a moment and glance at stage decoration generally. Here, too, in the matter of setting, naturalism was the prime objective. The first reaction occurred about 1890 and was instituted by a group of writers and artists termed *Symbolistes*, who were led by Paul Fort. They demanded the simplification of stage decoration, the abolition of the perspective back-cloth, and insisted on the harmonious co-ordination of costumes and setting, which must express the style-atmosphere of the play.

In Russia, a few years later, a similar contest was waged between realism in production—carried to the farthest extent in the Moscow Art Theatre, directed by Stanislavsky—and a new movement in the theatre sponsored by S. Mamontov, a rich Moscow manufacturer. Stanislavsky devoted his attention to the Drama; Mamontov's interest was centred on Opera, for the production of which he built himself a special theatre.

Mamontov was one of the great pioneers in securing recognition for Russian music, but his principal interest in relation to the subject of this introduction, is that he was perhaps the first person in Russia to form the conclusion that a stage setting could be something much more than a background for the actor or singer. He felt that scenery could be used to provide a beautiful picture, to evoke a fitting sense of style-atmosphere; and he was the first director to employ genuine artists such as Vasnetzov and Korovine to design the settings for his productions.

In 1899 Mamontov founded an art journal entitled *Mir Iskusstva* (*The World of Art*), of which the editor was Serge Diaghilev, and whose staff and contributors included Alexandre Benois, Bakst, Korovine, Serov, and others. These painters, although not professional designers for the stage, had an intense love of the theatre, which led them actively to promote the reform of stage decoration, not only by championing the cause in their journal, but by actual work in the theatre secured to some extent through Diaghilev's influence.

On July 22nd of the same year Prince Serge Wolkonsky was appointed director of the Imperial Theatres. He commissioned Golovine and Korovine to design settings for the ballets *Le Lac des Cygnes*, *Don Quichotte*, and *Le Miroir Magique*. He also attached Diaghilev to the directorate as an official for special missions and, when it was decided to revive Delibes's *Sylvia*, entrusted him with the artistic direction of the ballet. It was to have had settings and costumes by a combined group of artists—Benois, Bakst, Korovine, Lanceray, and Serov. Unfortunately, Diaghilev quarrelled with Prince Wolkonsky and resigned. Soon afterwards the director himself resigned owing to a difference with Kshesinskaya, the *prima ballerina assoluta*.

Wolkonsky was succeeded by Teliakovsky, who also gave opportunities to rising young painters, including Bakst, who, in 1902, made his *début* as stage designer with his setting for a version of Euripides's *Hippolytus*, and was next commissioned to design the setting and costumes for *Puppen-Fee*, an old German ballet which, later, tricked out in new guise, became *La Boutique Fantasque*.

In 1906, Diaghilev began his crusade of showing Russian art to Western Europe, as represented by Paris. He opened his campaign with an exhibition of painting of both the classical and modern schools, which was followed by a series of concerts of Russian music (1907), presentations of Russian opera (1908), and, finally, peformances of Russian ballet, as interpreted in the new school founded by Michel Fokine (1909). The ballets chosen had settings and costumes variously designed by Benois, Bakst, and Roehrich. Although the work of these three artists differs entirely, they are united by one common characteristic—acute feeling for mood and style-atmosphere, expressed in colour, form, and design.

If the reader will examine specimens of the work of these three painters of that period, it will be observed that the old theories of naturalism and perspective are rejected. There are no longer gigantic interiors and landscapes, laboriously constructed to resemble as nearly as possible the actual thing; on the contrary, the scenes suggest large-scale water-colours in which harmoniously clad figures dance and mime.

This double revelation of new thought in ballet production and the new school of stage decoration made an extraordinary impression on the spectators[1], particularly on those who practised the arts. Ballet, which had begun to grow jaded and seemingly incapable of further progress, was offered a new and unsuspected world of endeavour. There can be no doubt that the new stage decoration promoted a revolution in scenic art, whose influence still endures.

It is of interest to examine briefly the qualities of those painters who contributed so much to the success of Diaghilev's first season of ballet.

Benois' art is distinguished by a particular sense of aristocratic refinement; he has the fantasy of Berain[2] allied to the delicate colour sense of Bocquet,[3] and is seen at his best in designs associated

---

[1] The possibilities of the new school of stage decoration had been partly revealed in the staging of the operas presented by Diaghilev in 1908.

[2] Jean Berain (b. 1638), one of the most important French decorative artists of the 17th century. Under Louis XIV was *Dessinateur de la Chambre et du Cabinet du Roi,* and designed all costumes and properties required in connection with the festivals and entertainments given by the King.

[3] One of the most important French designers of costumes and settings for opera and ballet during the reign of Louis XV. Bocquet designed most of the costumes for Court entertainments given from 1763-1776.

with the 18th century, a period for which he has a particular regard.

Roehrich's work has a rugged primitiveness at once savage and grandiose which makes him an ideal designer for the evocation of early times.

Bakst was a master of the difficult art of blending colour, and he arranged his palette as a composer selects his key. In his hands colour could be as potent as a drug. Pink cloys, one shade of green soothes, another jars, one tone of red maddens, black and white depress, white purifies and chills—so Bakst played on the spectator's sense to induce a mood in harmony with the ballet. He could be romantic as in *Le Carnaval*; sensuous, almost erotic, as in *Schéhérazade*; mystical, as in *Le Dieu Bleu*; barbaric, as in *Thamar*; and lyrical as in *Narcisse*.

Russian painters—with the single exception of J. M. Sert—continued to provide the settings for the Diaghilev Company until 1917, and there were several additions to the original group, for instance, Dobuzhinsky, Goncharova, and Larionov. The colour note was continually heightened to reach its peak with Goncharova's setting for *Le Coq d'Or* (1914), in which certain scenes, conceived in the spirit of decoration of early Russian chap-books, were overwhelming in their effect. This purely Russian form of decoration was continued with great success by Larionov in *The Midnight Sun* (1915), *Contes Russes* (1917), and finally in *Chout* (1921), but, in the last-named work, the colour contrast was too strident and inclined to reduce the choreography to a subordinate position.

From 1917 onwards, with a few exceptions, Diaghilev selected his designers from modernist painters of easel pictures such as Derain, Matisse, Laurencin, Braque, Gris, Bauchant, and Rouault; or from advance-guard artists like Picasso, Ernst, Miro, Gabo, Pevsner, Tchelichev, and De Chirico. There was that one final orgy of colour in *Chout* and then the virile hues of the Russian decorators gave place to the pale, clear tints inaugurated by Picasso, slowly to descend the colour scale until they reached the whites and greys of the costumes in *Ode*.

There were many excellent settings achieved during this period, such as Bakst's evocation of Longhi and Guardi in *The Good Humoured Ladies*, Derain's *Boutique Fantasque*, Picasso's settings for *Le Tricorne* and *Pulcinella*, Bakst's essay in the grand manner, *The Sleeping Princess*, which recalled the Bibienas, Laurencin's *Les Biches*, and Pruna's *Les Matelots*.

The second decade of the Diaghilev Company was rich in experiment, for it included *Parade*, the first ballet to have a cubist setting, which was designed by Picasso; *Noces*, with its bleak and sober setting by Goncharova; three ballets with constructivist settings, *Le Pas d'Acier*, *La Chatte*, and *Ode;* and *Le Bal*, in which De Chirico made use of architectural motifs in both setting and costumes.

But the Diaghilev organisation was not the only company to contribute to the advancement of stage decoration. In 1920 another troupe, known as the *Ballets Suédois*, was formed by Rolf de Maré; this company consisted of Swedish and Danish dancers with Jean Borlin, a young Swedish dancer, as choreographer.

This company endured for five years, during which period twenty-two ballets were produced and shown to the principal cities of Europe and America. Many of those ballets were presented with an artistry of stage decoration equal to those of the better known Diaghilev company.

The first productions of the *Ballets Suédois* were decorated by Swedish painters such as Nils Dardel and Einar Nerman. Gradually, however, in the director's attempt to discover new paths for the development of ballet, the most modernist painters were commissioned to design settings, some of which mark a definite stage in the decoration of ballet. Take, for instance, *Skating Rink* and *La Création du Monde*, both designed by the cubist painter, Fernand Léger; then the unusual setting by Andrée Parr for Claudel's philosophic ballet, *L'Homme et son Désir*; and the very advanced *Relâche*, with setting by Picabia. This last was more iconoclastic even than anything attempted by Diaghilev.

Diaghilev died in 1929 and his troupe was disbanded. Towards 1932 the nucleus of a new company began to form at Monte Carlo under the joint management of Col. W. de Basil and René Blum. This troupe was known as *Les Ballets Russes de Monte Carlo*. Later the directors parted and two companies were formed, respectively known as *Les Ballets Russes de Col. de Basil* and *Les Ballets de Monte Carlo*, the latter directed by René Blum.

The first of these two companies acquired a number of the Diaghilev ballets which were revived with the original settings, or others based on the original productions, and, in addition, many new ballets were produced for which the following painters contributed designs: Cecil Beaton, the Comte de Beaumont, Christian Bérard, Raoul Dufy, André Derain, Alice Halicka, Jean Hugo, E. Lourie, André Masson, Joan Miro, and C. Terechkovich. The most successful of these designs is Miro's *surréaliste* setting for *Jeux d'Enfants*.

M. Blum has had the artistic collaboration of Dobuzhinsky for his revival of *Coppelia*, of Derain for his production of Fokine's

L'Epreuve d'Amour, and of the Catalan painter, Andreu, for his productions of Fokine's *Don Juan* and *Jota Aragonesa*.

The Soviet Ballet, which suggests an illimitable field for experiment, has contributed little to the advancement of stage decoration, with the exception of the very interesting experiments in constructivism attempted by Anatol Petritsky at Kharkov. The decoration of most of the ballets presented at Moscow and Leningrad is frankly realistic, and frequently of no particular distinction. Here I should like to make an exception in favour of Bobyshov, Dimitriev, and Rabinovich.

The ballet company attached to the Paris Opera has shown signs of renewed activity since Serge Lifar became *maitre de ballet*. Three productions at least are of great interest—*Sur le Borysthène*, with settings and costumes by Goncharova and Larionov (1932), *Icare*, with settings and costumes by Larthe (1935), and *David Triomphant*, with settings and costumes by Fernand Léger (1937).

From a choreographic standpoint one of the most interesting of recent ballets is *The Green Table* produced by Kurt Jooss at Paris in 1932. But, apart from the excellent masks designed by Hein Heckroth, it is not specially important from the decorative aspect, since, like most of Jooss's productions, it is given against a black velvet surround, the several changes being indicated by skilful lighting.

The Royal Danish Ballet has produced several ballets which are of particular artistic interest, for instance, *Bolero*, with setting and costumes by Svend Johannsen, and *La Veuve dans le Miroir*, with setting and costumes by Kjeld Abell.

At Budapest the settings for the productions of the Royal Hungarian Opera Ballet have been mainly designed by Gusztav Olah and Zoltan Fülöp, two artists endowed with unusually fertile imaginations and a rare feeling for design and decoration.

In Czechoslovakia there have been some unusual productions such as the *surréaliste* ballet *Songes*, with choreography by Milea Mayerova.

Italy has produced little experiment in modern forms. The most important settings have been those designed for the Scala Theatre, Milan, by the Italian painters Prince Mario Filomarino and Antonio Rovescalli, and the Russian, Nicholas Benois, and those designed by the first-named for the ballets given at the Royal Theatre, Rome, and the San Carlo Theatre, Naples, directed by Dr. Paolo Fabbri. The Chamber Ballet of San Remo, directed by Cia Fornaroli, presented settings planned for the miniature stage.

In the United States of America there has been a revival of interest in Ballet, and many of the productions of the last few years, particularly those sponsored by Adolph Bolm, the Chicago Opera Co., Michel Fokine, the Metropolitan Opera Co., and the Philadelphia Opera Co., have frequently been distinguished for their settings, for which, until recently, Russian artists resident in America, such as Remisov and Sudeikin, were mainly responsible.

But the determined effort to found a national ballet—a movement which had its inception in 1933 and the honour of which belongs to Lincoln Kirstein and Edward M. Warburg—has resulted in a new series of productions often remarkable for the artistry of their settings and costumes, which have been entrusted for the most part to modern French and Russian painters. Although the American Ballet has been but a comparatively short time in existence it can quote an imposing list of artists connected with its ballets—Bérard, Derain, Chaney, Halicka, Held, Lurçat, Sharaff, Sudeikin, Tchelichev, and Franklin Watkins.

In England, among the first modern English painters to design scenery for ballet were Albert Rutherston and S. H. Sime, both of whom contributed settings and costumes for the Pavlova Company; George Sheringham, who devised the dresses for *The Swinburne Ballet* (1917); Paul Nash, who designed the setting and costumes for Barrie's play with ballet—*The Truth about the Russian Dancers* (1920); and C. Lovat Fraser, who planned several costumes for Mme. Karsavina's season at the Coliseum (1921).

The foundation of the Camargo Society in 1931 not only gave an impetus to the development of English choreographers and dancers, but afforded native-born artists an opportunity of designing for the Ballet. Although the Society expired in 1933 it can look back upon a period of undoubted service towards the promotion of English Ballet and can cite an interesting selection of painters associated with its productions, for instance, John Armstrong, Vanessa Bell, Edward Burra, William Chappell, Duncan Grant, Gwendolen Raverat, and George Sheringham.

The establishment of the Vic-Wells Ballet by Lilian Baylis and Ninette de Valois in 1931, and that of the Ballet Club by Mme. Rambert in the same year, provided what it is to be hoped will prove to be permanent centres of Ballet in this country. Both directors have chosen their artistic collaborators with care, and many artistically interesting productions have been given by these two companies. The principal designers associated with the Vic-Wells ballet are John Armstrong, Cecil Beaton, Lord Berners, Hedley Briggs, William Chappell, Phyllis Dolton, Sophie Fedorovich, Motley,

Hugh Stevenson, and Rex Whistler; while the artists associated with the Ballet Club include Nadia Benois, William Chappell, Sophie Fedorovich, Andrée Howard, Susan Salaman, and Hugh Stevenson.

The recently formed Markova-Dolin Company has provided a further opportunity for designers for the Ballet and has already produced at least three scenically interesting works in Meninsky's settings and costumes for *David*, those of Motley for *Aucassin and Nicolette*, and those by Kirsta for *La Bien Aimée*.

* * *

What is the function of the stage setting in relation to Ballet? Primarily it is a background for the dancer, but that setting has to suggest the period, the place, and, most important of all, the mood of the ballet. And so the scene is invested with meaning by the application of form, decorative design, and colour.

Ballet is a complex art not fully savoured unless allied to its sister arts of music and painting, and the success of the complete work depends a great deal on the value of their co-operation, for inartistic scenery or costumes can mar a ballet just as much as poor choreography or bad dancing.

In general, the ideal scene is a painted back-cloth used in conjunction with suitable wings or cut-cloths, for this permits the attainment of the highest degree of poetic illusion, an essential quality, for the world of ballet is the domain of the unreal, and this type of setting frees the greatest area of the stage, an important consideration where dancing is concerned.

The scene can also take part in the ballet, for instance, the lines of the design can be repeated in the movements of the dancers. In the same way the scene can be used to reduce the dancers in size or, alternatively, accord them added height. The setting can concentrate attention on the dancer by throwing her into relief, or, failing sufficient contrast between costume and setting, reduce her to semi-obscurity.

There is a growing tendency in some quarters to make the setting felt rather than seen, to use a back-cloth in which decorative design is reduced to a minimum, the cloth being painted in one flat tone, or a succession of broken tones, sometimes in shades of the same colour, sometimes in two or three contrasted tints. This is the type of setting used in *Le Tricorne*, *Choreartium*, *Symphonie Fantastique*, and in many of the settings by Fedorovich seen at Sadler's Wells.

Costume for ballet is governed by five considerations: line, decorative design, colour, material, and relation to the dancer's movements. Again, the designer must always bear in mind that the costume worn by a dancer will be seen mainly under conditions of movement and, frequently, in very rapid movement.

For a work conceived in the style of the pure classical ballet, the ballet-skirt, pink tights, and satin shoes are *de rigueur*, and, if it be desired to suggest a particular period or setting, it is possible to introduce appropriate variations in cut and design which, in the hands of a skilful artist, can be very attractive. Admittedly the use of ballet-shoes with dresses of certain epochs can strike a discordant note, but, since certain forms of traditional technique depend on the ballet-shoe, a concession must be made to a convention born of necessity.

When the ballet has an element of national dancing, there are splendid opportunities to contrive costumes suggesting national dress. Examples of such types are found in *Petrouchka*, *Le Tricorne*, *La Jarre*, *La Nuit de St. Jean*, and so forth.

Abstract and modernist ballets offer the designer a wide field for experimental form and design.

Costume can play a considerable part in a ballet; it can assist the dancer in the creation of a character, emphasise line, and confer strength or softness according to its cut and material. Even a comparatively insignificant article of dress such as the white gloves worn by Chiarina and her friends in the *pas de trois* " *Chopin* " in Fokine's *Le Carnaval* can become so important that the dance is ruined if the gloves be made of another colour.

Further, the dancer's costume must be designed with a view not only to the theme and period of the ballet, but in relation to what the dancer is required to do, for a costume made of unsuitable material can make the dancer as leaden-footed as a diver beneath the sea; a faulty sleeve will restrict a movement that should be full, or perhaps suggest the defect of raised shoulders; while a badly-designed head-dress can prevent the execution of certain turning movements which depend on balance and control. These are merely a few examples by the way.

Of late years the vogue for athleticism has led to the theory that the best costume for the male dancer is none. One school prefers the dancer's dress to be reduced to the minimum compatible with decency, so that the costume consists of little more than abbreviated shorts combined with a vest or miniature cape flung over the shoulders; another school favours the fleshings borrowed from the acrobat. These types, used in moderation, have much to commend them, but, exploited to excess, they become tedious. Certainly the dancer attains an ideal quality of freedom in his movements, but not without a certain loss of effect, for the designer's invention is restricted, and the pleasing variety of shapes resulting from a well-planned costume is completely lost.

When the costumes have been roughed out, they must then be thought of in relation to the setting, so that one contributes to the other, while, together, they form an harmonious entity. Bakst, when designing a setting, used to say that it corresponded to a picture where the figures had still to be painted in.

The problem of establishing a nice balance between costume and setting is complicated in proportion to the number of costumes seen on the stage at one time, and according to their proximity or distance apart. Again, it is important to visualise the possible effect on the spectator of a costume or set of costumes, when followed, at a short interval, by another and different costume or set of costumes.

* * *

The possibilities of Ballet to-day are immense; it is a most adaptable medium. Even in the eighteenth century Noverre observed that " a *maitre de ballet* ought to explore everything, to examine all, since everything that exists in the universe can serve him as a model." And this dictum is truer still to-day when Ballet has become a vastly more comprehensive and more expressive art.

The steady growth of public interest has resulted in an increasing number of works being produced, particularly in England and America, a happy state of affairs which, if the promise be maintained, should afford designers a new field of endeavour; and, in the case of those who, by observation and study, have sought to fit themselves for the task, an opportunity to make their own contribution to the advancement of Ballet which, as already stated, is a composite branch of the Theatre in which choreography, music, *and painting* each and all play their part.

CYRIL W. BEAUMONT.

Tyl Eulenspiegel and *Ballade*

(By courtesy of Theatre Arts Monthly)

Robert Edmond Jones. Setting for " Tyl Eulenspiegel." Ballet with music by Richard Strauss ; choreography by Vaslav Nijinsky. Presented by the Diaghilev Ballet Co., New York, 1916.

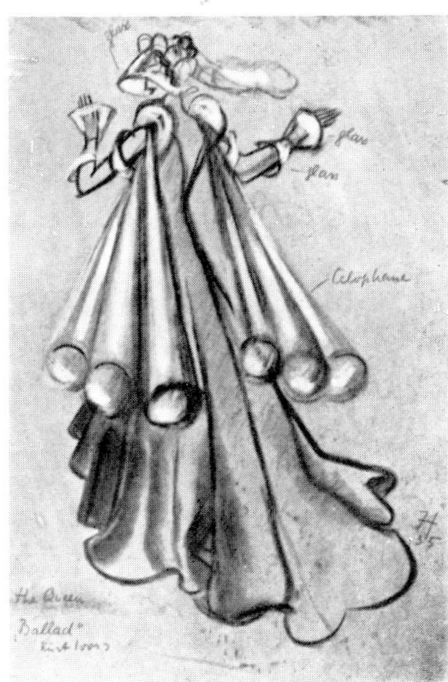

Hein Heckroth: Costumes for "Ballade." Ballet with music by Colman; choreography by Kurt Jooss. Presented by Ballets Jooss, Gaiety Theatre, London, 1935.

Le Coq d'Or

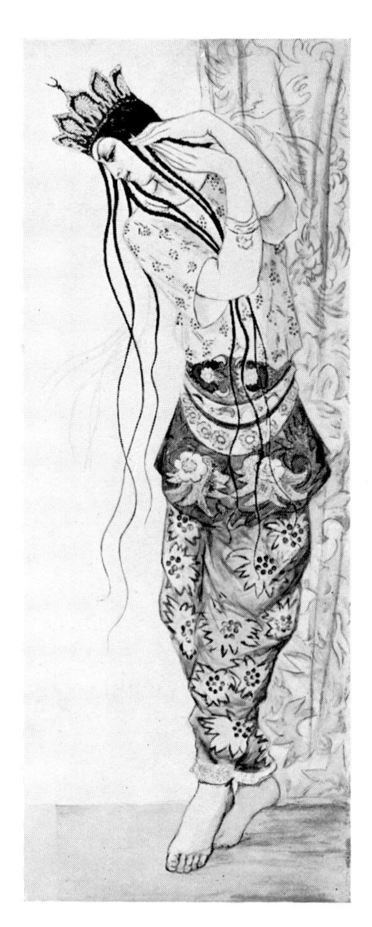

Natalia Goncharova. Costumes for "Le Coq d'Or"—Prince Guidon (left), and The Queen of Shemakhân (right).

Natalia Goncharova. Setting for "Le Coq d'Or," Act II, Scene I. Opera-ballet by V. Bielsky, music by N. Rimsky-Korsakov, choreography by Michel Fokine. Presented by the Diaghilev Ballet Co., Opéra, Paris, 1914.

Contes Russes

Michel Larionov. Setting for " Contes Russes " (Children's Tales), Act III. Ballet to music by Liadov, choreography by Leonide Massine. Presented by the Diaghilev Ballet, Théâtre du Chatelet, Paris, 1917.

Michel Larionov. Costumes for " Contes Russes "—Peasant (left), and a Wood-Demon (right).

El Greco and Offerlunden

Scene from "El Greco." Setting by Mouveau. Ballet with music by D. E. Inghelbrecht, choreography by Jean Borlin. Presented by Rolf de Maré's Ballets Suédois, Théâtre des Champs-Elysées, Paris, 1920.

Gunnar Hallstroem. Setting for "Offerlunden." Ballet with music by Algot Haquinius, choreography by Jean Borlin. Presented by Rolf de Maré's Ballets Suédois, Théâtre des Champs-Elysées, Paris, 1923.

The Birthday of the Infanta

Robert Edmond Jones. Setting for "The Birthday of the Infanta," Scene II. Ballet based on story by Oscar Wilde, music by J. A. Carpenter, choreography by Adolph Bolm. Presented by Chicago Opera Association, 1920.

Boite a Joujoux

André Hellé. Setting and costumes for "Boîte à Joujoux". Ballet with music by Claude Debussy, choreography by Jean Borlin. Presented by Rolf de Maré's Ballets Suédois, Théâtre des Champs-Elysées, Paris, 1920.

Pierre Laprade. Setting for " Le Tombeau de Couperin." Ballet with music by Ravel, choreography by Jean Borlin. Presented by Rolf de Maré's Ballets Suédois, Théâtre des Champs-Elysées, Paris, 1920.

Pierre Laprade. Costumes for " Le Tombeau de Couperin."

Les Vierges Folles

Einar Nerman. Setting and costumes for "Les Vierges Folles." Ballet by K. Atterberg and E. Nerman, music by K. Atterberg, choreography by Jean Borlin. Presented by Rolf de Maré's Ballets Suédois, Théâtre des Champs-Elysées, Paris, 1920.

Paul Coln. Setting for "Sculpture Nègre." Dance executed and arranged by Jean Borlin.

Andrée Parr. Setting for "L'Homme et son Désir." Plastic Poem by Paul Claudel, music by Darius Milhaud, choreography by Jean Borlin. Presented by Rolf de Maré's Ballets Suédois, Théâtre des Champs-Elysées, Paris, 1921.

Andrée Parr. Costumes for "L'Homme et Son Désir." Plastic Poem by Paul Claudel, music by Darius Milhaud, choreography by Jean Borlin. Presented by Rolf de Maré's Ballets Suédois, Théâtre des Champs-Elysées, Paris, 1921.

Léon Bakst. Costumes for "The Sleeping Princess"—The Porcelain Princesses, showing adaptation of 18th century conception of Chinese costumes. Ballet by Marius Petipa, music by P. I. Tchaikovsky, choreography by Marius Petipa. Revival, as presented by the Diaghilev Ballet Co., Alhambra Theatre, London, 1921.

Photos: Stage Photo Co.

Léon Bakst. Costumes for "The Sleeping Princess"—Scheherazade, The Shah, and his Brother, showing adaptation of Persian costumes.

Photos: Stage Photo Co.

Léon Bakst. Animal Costumes for "The Sleeping Princess"—Carabosse, surrounded by her Rats. Notice the gauze-covered vent in the rats' muzzles, which enables the dancer to see and breathe.

Léon Bakst. Animal Costumes for "The Sleeping Princess"—The Wolf (left), The White Cat and Puss-in-Boots (right).

Chout

Michel Larionov. Setting for "Chout" (The Buffoon), Scene II. Ballet with music by S. Prokofiev, choreography by T. Slavinsky and M. Larionov. Presented by the Diaghilev Ballet Co., Paris, 1921.

Michel Larionov. Costumes for "Chout"—The Buffoon (left) and The Merchant (right).

Jean Hugo. Costumes for "Les Mariés de la Tour Eiffel." Ballet by Jean Cocteau, music by The Six, choreography by Jean Borlin. Presented by Rolf de Maré's Ballets Suédois, Théâtre des Champs-Elysées, Paris, 1921. Top—The Ostrich (left), The Bathing-Girl from Trouville (right). Below—The General (left), The Photographer (right).

Michel Larionov. Setting for "Renard." Ballet with theme and music by I. Stravinsky. Second version, with choreography by Serge Lifar. Presented by the Diaghilev Ballet Co., Théâtre Sarah Bernhardt, Paris, 1929. (Below) Natalia Goncharova. Costume for "Renard," 1922 production—The Fox. Michel Larionov. Costume for "Renard," 1922 production—The Cock.

Renard and *La Foire de Sorochinsk*

Michel Larionov. Setting for "Renard." Ballet with theme and music by I. Stravinsky. First version, with choreography by Bronislava Nijinska. Presented by Diaghilev Ballet Co., Opéra, Paris, 1922. (In the collection of A. Tomiline, Paris.)

Natalia Goncharova. Act-drop for "La Foire de Sorochinsk." Opera-ballet with music by Mussorgsky. Presented by Opéra et Ballet Privés de Paris, Théâtre des Champs-Elysées, 1926. (In the collection of O. Rosenfeld, Paris.)

Scenes from " L'Oiseau de Feu." Settings and costumes designed by Natalia Goncharova. Originally produced for the Diaghilev Ballet Co., 1922. These photographs are from the revival, as now presented by Col. W. de Basil's Ballets Russes. Ballet by Michel Fokine, music by Igor Stravinsky, choreography by M. Fokine.

Skating Rink

Fernand Léger. Cubist setting and costumes for "Skating Rink." Ballet by R. Canudo, music by A. Honegger, choreography by Jean Borlin. Presented by Rolf de Maré's Ballets Suédois, Theâtre des Champs-Elysées, Paris, 1922.

Fernand Léger. Costumes and Cubist Setting for "La Création du Monde." Ballet by B. Cendrars, music by Darius Milhaud, choreography by Jean Borlin. Presented by Rolf de Maré's Ballets Suédois, Théâtre des Champs Elysées, Paris, 1923.

Marchand d'Oiseaux

Hélène Perdriat. Setting for "Marchand D'Oiseaux." Ballet with music by Germaine Tailleferre, choreography by Jean Borlin. Presented by Rolf de Maré's Ballets Suédois, Théâtre des Champs-Elysées, Paris, 1923. Below, two costumes for "Marchand D'Oiseaux"—The Bird Vendor (left), The Younger Sister (right).

Les Maries de la Tour Eiffel and La Jarre

Irène Lagut. Back-cloth for "Les Mariés de la Tour Eiffel." Ballet by Jean Cocteau, music by The Six, choreography by Jean Borlin. Presented by Rolf de Maré's Ballets Suédois, Théâtre des Champs-Elysées, Paris, 1921.

Giorgio de Chirico. Setting for "La Jarre." Ballet by L. Pirandello, music by A. Casella, choreography by Jean Borlin. Presented by Rolf de Maré's Ballets Suédois, Théâtre des Champs-Elysées, Paris, 1924.

Within the Quota

GEM ROBBERS FOIL $210,000 SWINDLE

EXTRA

Largest Liner In

THE WEATHER

NEW YORK CHICAGOA DAILY

FINAL EDITION

Ex-Wife's Heart-Balm Love-Tangle

UNKNOWN BANKER BUYS ATLANTIC

RUM RAID LIQUOR BAN

ROMANCE ENDS IN COURT

Auto King Pledge Boom

MAMMOTH PLANE UP

THRONGS AT DEAL SHOE-MAGNATE PARTY SPLIT

BOYCOTT ALL SYNDICATE HOOTCH

PITTSBURGH : 0100
WASHINGTON : 1010
Scott and Agnew; Kip, Ho.
PORTLAND : 1002
SEATTLE : 0110

CATANIA, June 19.—Molten lava to-day destroyed the village of Cazamica, near the foot of Mount Etna.

LONDON, June 19.—Activity of Mount Etna again increased this afternoon.

Gerald Murphy. Setting and Costumes for "Within the Quota." The setting is a giant reproduction of an American "daily." The characters represented are The Coloured Gentleman, The Immigrant, The World's Sweetheart, The Cow-boy. Ballet by G. Murphy, music by Cole Porter, choreography by Jean Borlin. Presented by Rolf de Maré's Ballets Suédois, Théâtre des Champs-Elysées, Paris, 1923

Noces

Natalia Goncharova. Setting for "Noces," Scene III, and two costumes. The men and women dancers each wear a stylised peasant dress of uniform design. Ballet with theme and music by I. Stravinsky. Presented by the Diaghilev Ballet Co., Gaîté-Lyrique, Paris, 1923.

Scene from " Le Train Bleu." Setting by H. Laurens. Costumes by Chanel. Ballet by Jean Cocteau, music by Darius Milhaud, choreography by Bronislava Nijinska. Presented by the Diaghilev Ballet Co., Théâtre des Champs-Elysées, Paris, 1924.

Photos: The Times, London

Scene from " Les Biches." Setting and costumes by Marie Laurencin. Ballet with music by Francis Poulenc, choreography by Bronislava Nijinska. Presented by the Diaghilev Ballet Co., Théâtre de Monte Carlo, 1924.

Relache

Francis Picabia. Setting for "Relâche." Ballet by F. Picabia, music by Erik Satie, production by F. Picabia, choreography by Jean Borlin. Presented by Rolf de Maré's Ballets Suédois, Théâtre des Champs-Elysées, Paris, 1924. Below—Curtain for "Relâche." The names were painted in transparent colours, lit from behind, and made to flicker by inserting a flasher in the electric circuit, thus giving the effect of electric night-signs.

Anatol Petritsky. Setting for "Le Corsaire" and costume (Medora). Ballet by Saint-Georges and Mazilier, music by Adam, choreography by Mazilier. Revival, presented by Soviet State Ballet, Kharkov, 1925.

Les Tentations de la Bergere and Aucassin and Nicolette

Photo : Ernest H. Mills

Scene from "Les Tentations de la Bergère." Setting and Costumes by Juan Gris. Ballet with music by Monteclair, choreography by Bronislava Nijinska. Presented by the Diaghilev Ballet Co., Théâtre de Monte Carlo, 1924.

Photo : Sasha

Scene from "Aucassin and Nicolette." Setting and costumes by Motley. Ballet with music by Joseph Holbrook, choreography by Wendy Toye. Presented by Markova-Dolin Ballet 1936.

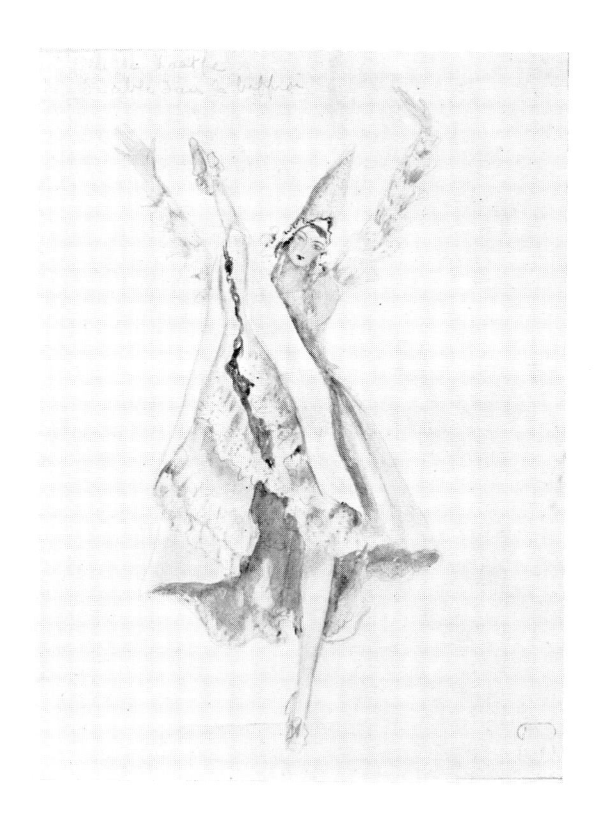

Per Krocht. Scene Model for "Le Diable dans le Beffroi," and costumes—Jo, Kaatje's Daughter (left), A Youth (right). Ballet with choreography by Nicholas Guerra. Presented at Opéra, Paris, 1927. (By courtesy of the Musée de l'Opéra, Paris).

La Chatte

Photo : Sasha, London

Scene and costumes from "La Chatte." Constructivist Setting by Gabo and Pevsner. The scenery and costumes are made of talc, a material with many attractive possibilities on account of its lightness, transparency, flexibility, and power to reflect light. Ballet by Sobeka, music by Henri Sauguet, choreography by George Balanchine. Presented by the Diaghilev Ballet Co., Prince's Theatre, London, 1927.

Photo : Henri Manuel, Paris

Photo: Lipnitzki, Paris

Violin costume in " L'Orchestre en Liberté."

Jean Berain. Costume for a Musician. Example of 17th century treatment of musical instruments as decorative elements for a dancer's costume.

Nicholas Remisov. Costume for a Violin in " The Tragedy of the Cello."

Nicholas Remisov. Setting for " The Tragedy of the Cello." Ballet with music by A. Tansman, choreography by Adolph Bolm, 1927.

The Nightingale and the Rose

Phyllis Dolton. Setting and costumes for "The Nightingale and the Rose." Music by H. Fraser Simson, choreography by Anton Dolin. Presented by Nemchinova-Dolin Ballet, Coliseum Theatre, London, 1927.

Costume for The Student.

Costume for The Nightingale

Photo: Richard Tucker, Boston

Scene from "Apollon Musagète." Setting and costumes by André Bauchant. Ballet with music by I. Stravinsky, choreography by George Balanchine. Presented by the Diaghilev Ballet Co., His Majesty's Theatre, London, 1928.

Scene from "Apollon Musagète." Setting and Costumes by Stewart Chaney. Ballet with music by I. Stravinsky, choreography by George Balanchine. Presented by American Ballet, New York, 1937.

Photo: The Times, London

Costumes by Alexandre Benois

Alexandre Benois. (Above.) Costumes for "La Bien Aimée." Ballet by A. Benois, music by Schubert and Liszt, choreography by Bronislava Nijinska. Presented by Ballet Ida Rubinstein, Opéra, Paris, 1928.

(Below.) Costumes for "Les Noces de Psyche et l'Amour." Ballet with music by Bach, choreography by Bronislava Nijinska. Presented by Ballet Ida Rubinstein, Opéra, Paris, 1928.

Alexandre Benois. Setting for "Les Noces de Psyche et L'Amour."—Apotheosis. Ballet to music by Bach, choreography by Bronislava Nijinska. Presented by Ballet Ida Rubinstein, Opéra, Paris, 1928.

Alexandre Benois. Curtain for "Le Coq D'Or.' Presented at Opéra, Paris, 1927.

Alexandra Benois. Setting for " Sadko."

Alexandre Benois. Setting for " La Princesse Cygne." Ballet with music by Rimsky-Korsakov, choreography by Bronislava Nijinska. Presented by Ballet Ida Rubinstein, Opéra, Paris, 1928.

Sadko

Sergey Sudeikine. Setting and Costumes for "Sadko," Act III, Scene II—"Beneath the Sea." The Costumes represented are Seaweed (centre), Ocean Wave (left), and Pearls (right). Opera ballet by N. Rimsky-Korsakov. Presented at Metropolitan Opera House, New York.

William Chappell. Costumes for "Capriol Suite." Ballet to music by Peter Warlock, choreography by Frederick Ashton. Presented by Ballet Rambert, Lyric Theatre, Hammersmith, 1930.

William Chappell. Costume for "Bar Aux Folies Bergères"—The Barmaid. Ballet to music by Chabrier, choreography by Ninette de Valois. Presented by Ballet Rambert, Mercury Theatre, London, 1934.

Costume for "Lysistrata"—A Wife. Ballet to music by S. Prokofiev, choreography by Antony Tudor. Presented by Ballet Rambert, Mercury Theatre, London, 1932.

Le Rustre Imprudent and La Jarre

Charles Martin. Costumes for "Le Rustre Imprudent." Ballet with choreography by Leo Staats. Presented at Opéra, Paris, 1931. (By courtesy of the Musée de l'Opéra).

Giorgio de Chirico. Costumes for "La Jarre." Ballet by L. Pirandello, music by A. Casella, choreography by Jean Borlin. Presented by Rolf de Maré's Ballets Suédois, Théâtre des Champs-Elysées, Paris, 1924.

Costumes by Philip Gough

Philip Gough. (Above.) Costumes for " Fun in a Toy Shop "—Waltzing Doll and Clown. Ballets by Marjorie Field in " Children's Variety Show " presented at the Ambassador's Theatre, London, 1935. (Below.) Costumes for " The Masque of the Red Death "—A Gentleman of the Court and A Lady of the Court. Ballet with music by Cyril Scott, choreography by Quentin Tod, 1930.

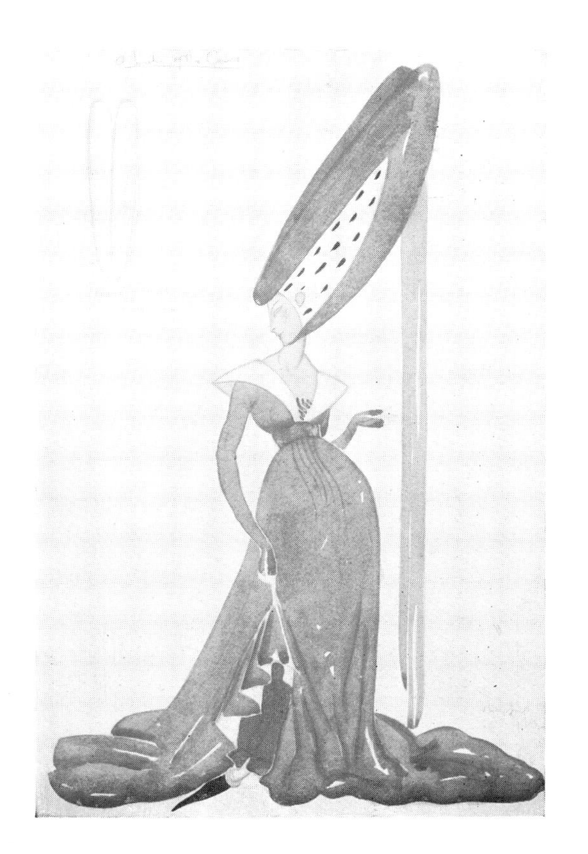

Khodasevich. Costumes for "Esmeralda," Act II, and setting for Act IV. Ballet by Jules Perrot, music by Pugni, choreography by Jules Perrot. Revival, as presented by Soviet State Ballet.

Hein Heckroth. Design for the masks to be worn by the diplomats in "The Green Table," and below, a Scene. Ballet by Kurt Jooss, music by F. A. Cohen, choreography by Kurt Jooss. Presented by Ballets Jooss, Paris, 1932.

The Red Poppy

Scenes from "The Red Poppy," Act III, Scene I, and, below, Act I. Ballet by M. T. Kurilko, music by R. M. Glière, choreography by F. V. Lopukhov. Presented by Soviet State Ballet.

Scenes from "Belkis, Queen of Sheba," Act II, and, below, Act I. Settings and costumes by Nicholas Benois. Ballet by C. Guastalla, music by O. Respighi, choreography by Leonide Massine. Presented at Scala Theatre, Milan, 1932.

Photos: Crimella, Milan.

Les Comediens Jaloux

Georges Annenkov. Settings for " Les Comédiens Jaloux." Scene II, and, below, Scene I. Ballet based on Moliere's play, with choreography by Bronislava Nijinska. Presented by La Nijinska's Théâtre de la Danse, Théâtre de l'Opéra Comique, Paris, 1932.

Georges Annenkov. Settings for " Variations," Part I, and, below, Part II. Ballet in 3 parts, with choreography by Bronislava Nijinska. Presented by La Nijinska's Théâtre de la Danse, Théâtre de l'Opéra Comique, Paris, 1932.

Sur le Borysthene

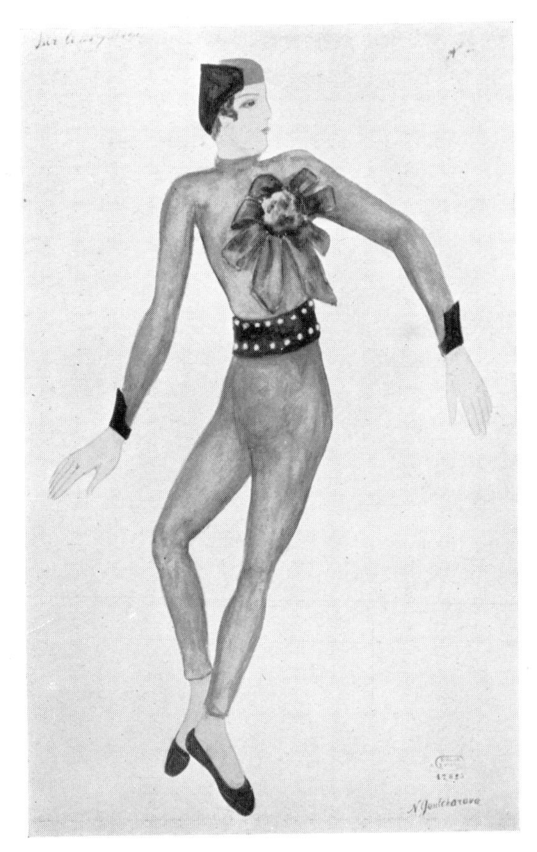

Michel Larionov. Scene model of constructivist setting for "Sur le Borysthène," with two costumes by Natalia Goncharova. Ballet with music by S. Prokofiev, choreography by Serge Lifar. Presented at the Opèra, Paris, 1932. (By courtesy of the Musée l'Opéra, Paris)

Photo: Raoul Barba, Monte Carlo

Scene from "Jeux d'Enfants." Setting and Costumes by Joan Miro. Ballet by B. Kochno, music by G. Bizet, choreography by Leonide Massine. Presented by Les Ballets Russes de Monte Carlo, Théâtre de Monte Carlo, 1932.

Photo: Lipnitzki, Paris

Scene from "Ode." Setting by Pavel Tchelitchev. Ballet by B. Kochno, music by N. Nabokov, choreography by Leonide Massine. Presented by the Diaghilev Ballet Co., His Majesty's Theatre, London, 1928.

The Flames of Paris

V. V. Dmitriev. Settings for "The Flames of Paris," Acts III and IV. Ballet by N. D. Volkov and V. V. Dmitriev, music by B. V. Asafiev, choreography by V. I. Vynonen. Presented by Soviet State Ballet, 1932.

Scenes from "Kuruc Fairy Tale," Act II, and, below, Act I. Settings and costumes designed by Gusztav Oláh. Ballet by Zsolt Harsányi, music by Zoltán Kodály, choreography by Aurel Millos and Rezsö Brada. Presented by Royal Hungarian State Ballet, Royal Opera House, Budapest, 1935.

Photos: Vajda M. Pal, Budapest

William Chappell. Costumes for "High Yellow." Ballet with music by Spike Hughes, choreography by Buddy Bradley and Frederick Ashton. Presented by Camargo Society, Savoy Theatre, London, 1932.

Vanessa Bell. Setting for "High Yellow." (In the collection of John V. Trevor.)

Gwendolen Raverat. Setting for "Job." Masque for Dancing by Geoffrey Keynes, music by Vaughan Williams, choreography by Ninette de Valois. Presented by Camargo Society, Cambridge Theatre, London, 1931. (In the collection of Geoffrey Keynes, Esq., London).

Nadia Benois. Setting for "Dark Elegies." Ballet to music by Mahler, choreography by Antony Tudor. Presented by Ballet Rambert, Duchess Theatre, London, 1937.

Costumes by Mitislav Dobuzhinsky

Mitislav Dobuzhinsky. (Above.) Two costumes for " La Belle au Bois Dormant "—A Duchess and The Blue Bird. Ballet by M. Petipa, music by P. I. Tchaikovsky, choreography by Marius Petipa. Revival, as presented by Lithuanian Ballet, Kovno. (Below.) Costume for " Prince Igor "—Polovtsian Dancer. Revival as presented by Lithuanian Ballet, Kovno. Costume for " La Belle au Bois Dormant "—Carabosse.

Danses Villageoises and Le Tricorne

Scene from "Danses Villageoises." Setting and Costumes by Prince Mario Cito Filomarino. Ballet with music by Grétry, choreography by Pratesi. Revival, as presented at Scala Theatre, Milan, 1933.

Photo: Crimella, Milan.

Scene from "Le Tricorne." Setting and Costumes by Prince Mario Cito Filomarino. Ballet with music by M. de Falla, choreography by Lizzie Maudrick. Presented at Scala Theatre, Milan, 1933.

The Selfish Giant and The Prince Carved From Wood

Scene from "The Selfish Giant" (Az Onzö Oriás). Setting and costumes by Zoltan Fülöp. Opera-ballet based on story by Oscar Wilde, music by Jenö von Hubay, choreography by Rezsö Brada. Presented by Royal Hungarian State Ballet, Royal Opera House, Budapest.

Photos: Vajda M. Pal, Budapest

Scene from "The Prince Carved From Wood" (Faból faragott királyfi). Setting and costumes designed by Gustav Oláh and Zoltan Fülöp, music by Béla Bartók, choreography by Jan Cieplinsky. Presented by Royal Hungarian State Ballet, Royal Opera House, Budapest, 1935.

The Birds

M. Vellani-Marchi. Setting for " The Birds." Ballet by C. Guastalla, music by O. Respighi, choreography by Cia Fornaroli) Presented by Italian Chamber Ballet, San Remo, 1933.

Titina Rota. Costumes for " The Birds."—The Cuckoo (left), The Cock (right).

Achille Broggi. Setting for "Berceuse." Ballet with music by Riccardo Pick-Mangiagalli, choreography by Cia Fornaroli. Presented by Italian Chamber Ballet, San Remo, 1933.

Titina Rota. Costumes for "Berceuse."

Le Mouvement and L'Homme et la Machine

Paul Colin. Setting for "Le Mouvement," suggested by units of machinery. Presented at Casino de Paris, Paris, 1933.

Paul Colin. Setting for "L'Homme et la Machine." Ballet presented at Casino de Paris, Paris, 1934.

Photo : Almberg & Preinitz, Stockholm

Jon Aud. Back-cloth for "Le Train Bleu." Ballet by Jean Cocteau, music by Darius Milhaud. Revival, as presented at Royal Opera House, Stockholm, 1934.

Scene from "Bolero." Setting and costumes by Svend Johannsen. Ballet to music by Ravel, choreography by Harold Lander. Presented at Theatre Royal, Copenhagen, 1934.

Les Masques

Sophie Fedorovich. Setting and costumes for "Les Masques." Ballet with music by Francis Poulenc, choreography by Frederick Ashton. Presented by Ballet Rambert, Mercury Theatre, London, 1933.

Photo : Raoul Barba, Monte Carlo

Scene from "Les Présages." Setting and costumes by André Masson. Ballet by L. Massine, music by P. I. Tchaikovsky, choreography by Leonide Massine. Presented by Les Ballets Russes de Monte Carlo, Théâtre de Monte Carlo, 1933.

Photo : Maurice Seymour, Chicago

Scene from "Choreartium." Settings and costumes by Constantin Terechkovich and Eugene Lourie. Ballet to music by Brahms, choreography by Leonide Massine. Presented by Les Ballets Russes de Monte Carlo, Alhambra Theatre, London, 1933.

Scuola di Ballo and Le Beau Danube

Scene from "Scuola di Ballo." Setting and costumes by the Comte Etienne de Beaumont. Ballet by L. Massine, music by Boccherini, choreography by Leonide Massine. Presented by Les Ballets Russes de Monte Carlo, Théâtre de Monte Carlo, 1933.

Photos: Raoul Barba, Monte Carlo

Scene from "Le Beau Danube." Setting by Vladimir Polunin after Constantin Guys. Ballet by L. Massine, music by Johann Strauss, choreography by Leonide Massine. Revival, as presented by Les Ballets Russes de Monte Carlo, 1933.

The Lord of Burleigh and Pan

George Sheringham. Setting for "The Lord of Burleigh." Ballet to music by Mendelssohn, choreography by Frederick Ashton. Presented by the Camargo Society, London, 1931. (In the collection of John V. Trevor).

George Sheringham. Setting for "Pan," ballet not yet given. (In the collection of Helen Gardiner, M.V.O., and Patience Osburn.)

The Three Fat Men

Two scenes from "The Three Fat Men," Act I, Scene II, and Act III, Scene I. Settings by B. A. Matrunin. Ballet by I. Olecha, music by V. A. Oransky, choreography by I. A. Moiseyev. Presented by Soviet State Ballet.

Two scenes from "Magyar Abrandok" (Hungarian Fantasy), Acts II and III. Setting and costumes by Zoltan Fülöp and Gusztav Olah, respectively. Ballet by L. Márkus, music by Liszt, choreography by Jan Cieplinsky. Presented by Royal Hungarian State Ballet, Royal Opera House, Budapest, 1933.

Photos: Vajda M. Pal, Budapest

Arlequinade

Mitislav Dobuzhinsky. Setting for "Arlequinade," and below, two costumes, for Harlequin (left) and Columbine (right). Ballet with music by Richard Drigo. Presented by Lithuanian Ballet, State Theatre, Kovno.

William Chappell. Back-cloth for "The Jar," and, below, two costumes, for Zi 'Dima (left) and Nela (right). Ballet by L. Pirandello, music by A. Casella, choreography by Ninette de Valois. Revival, as presented by Vic-Wells Ballet, Sadler's Wells Theatre, London, 1934.

Raymonda

Costume for Abderam.

Costume for Spanish Dance—Panaderos.

Mitislav Dobuzhinsky. Costume designs for Raymonda. Ballet by L. Pashkov and M. Petipa, music by A. Glazunov, choreography by Marius Petipa. Revival, as presented by Lithuanian State Ballet, Kovno, 1934.

Mitislav Dobuzhinsky. **Setting for "Raymonda."** Act I, Scene II

Motley. Setting for "The Haunted Ballroom," and costume (The Stranger Player). Ballet with music by Geoffrey Toye, choreography by Ninette de Valois. Presented by Vic-Wells Ballet, Sadler's Wells Theatre, London, 1934.

F. F. Fedorovsky. Costumes for the Polovtsian Dances in "Prince Igor." Opera by Borodine, production by Baratov. Presented at Bolshoy Theatre, Moscow, 1934.

Scene from "Prince Igor"—Polovtsian Dances. Setting by F. F. Fedorovsky.

Mermaid and Le Tricorne

Andrée Howard. Costumes for "Mermaid"—The Prince (left), Women (right). Ballet with music by Ravel, choreography by Andrée Howard and Susan Salaman. Presented by Ballet Rambert, Mercury Theatre, London, 1934.

Photo: A. J. Vaughan, London

Scene from "Le Tricorne" (The Three-Cornered Hat). Setting and costumes by Pablo Picasso. Ballet by Martinez Sierra, music by M. de Falla, choreography by Leonide Massine. Presented by Diaghilev Ballet Co., Alhambra Theatre, London, 1919.

Photo : J. W. Deoenham, London

Scene from "The Gods Go A-Begging." Setting and costumes by Hugh Stevenson. Ballet to music by Handel, arranged by Sir Thomas Beecham, choreography by Ninette de Valois. Presented by Vic-Wells Ballet, Sadler's Wells Theatre, London, 1934.

Photo : Raoul Barba, Monte Carlo

Scene from "Cotillon." Setting and costumes by Christian Bérard. Ballet with music by Chabrier, choreography by George Balanchine. Presented by Ballets Russes de Monte Carlo, Théâtre de Monte Carlo, 1932.

Hugh Stevenson. Two settings for " The Planets "—Venus and, below, Mars. Ballet with music by Gustav Holst, choreography by Antony Tudor. Presented by Ballet Rambert, Mercury Theatre, London, 1934.

Hugh Stevenson. Setting for "Kalevala." Ballet founded on the Finnish epic, with choreography by Antony Tudor (in preparation). Below, two costumes—The Chanters of the Runes.

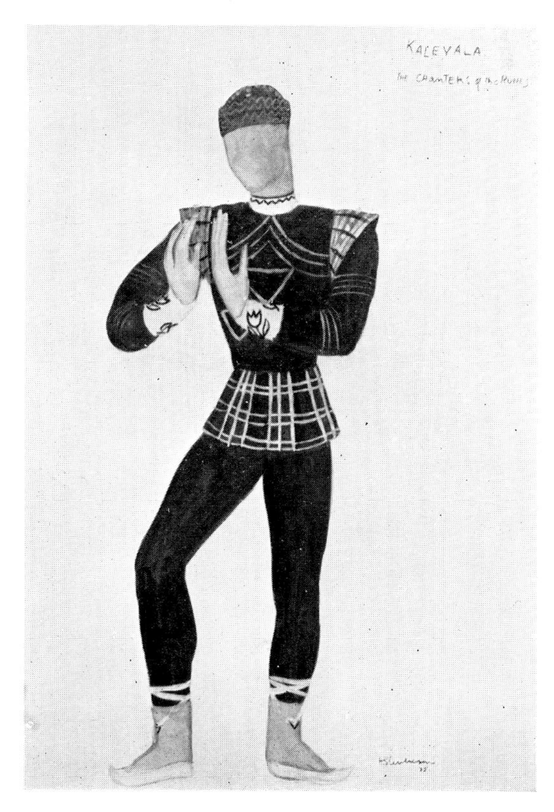

The Fountain of Bakhchisaray

V. M. Khodasevich. Setting for " The Fountain of Bakhchisaray," Act II, and two costumes—Gierey (left), and Zarema (right). Ballet by N. D. Volkov, music by B. V. Asafiev, production by R. V. Zakharov. Presented by Soviet State Ballet.

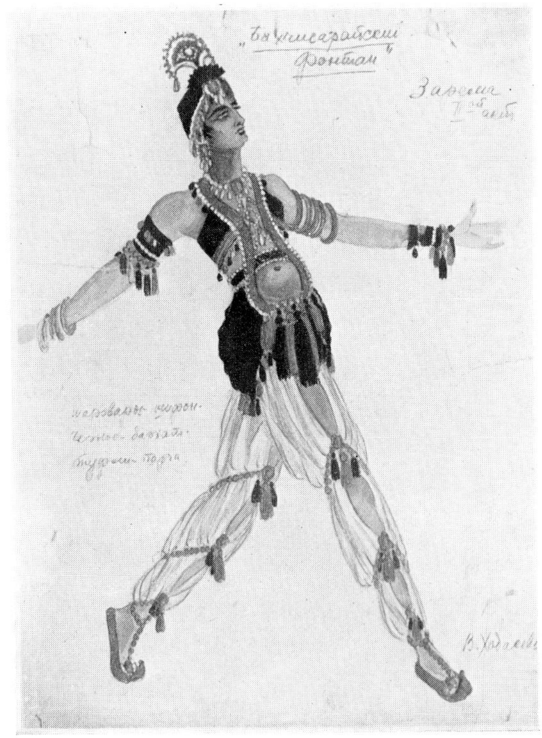

The Descent of Hebe

Nadia Benois. Setting for "The Descent of Hebe," and two costumes—Hercules (left), Hebe (right). Ballet by A. Tudor, music by Ernest Bloch, choreography by Antony Tudor. Presented by Ballet Rambert, Mercury Theatre, London, 1935.

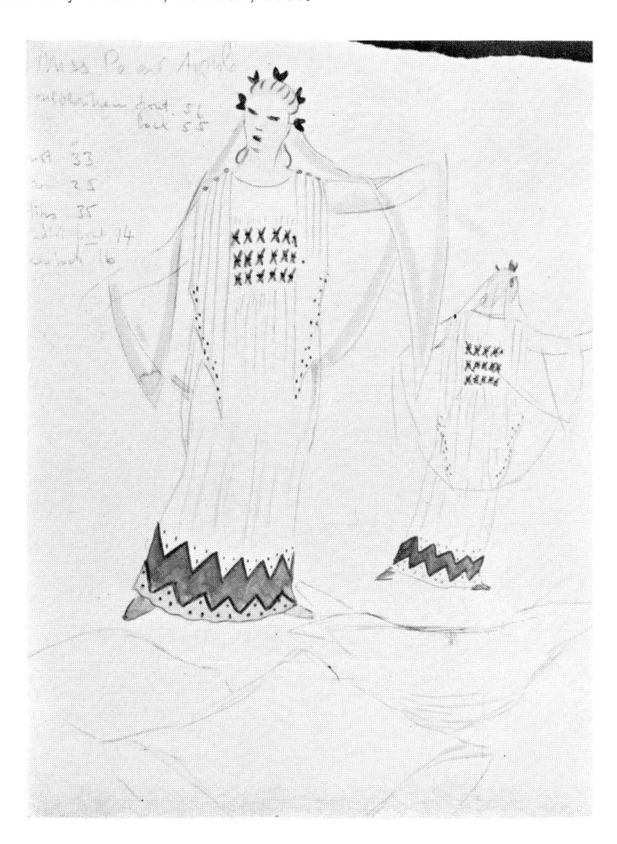

Mephisto Valse and Le Baiser de la Fee

Sophie Fedorovich. Costumes for " Mephisto Valse "—Mephisto (left), Marguerite (right). Ballet with music by Liszt, choreography by Frederick Ashton. Presented by Ballet Rambert, Duke of York's Theatre, London, 1935.

Scene from " Le Baiser de la Fée." Setting by Bassadoua. Ballet with music by I. Stravinsky, choreography by Bronislava Nijinska. Presented at Colon Theatre, Buenos Aires, 1932.

Giselle

William Chappell. Project for setting for "Giselle," and two costumes—Prince Albrecht (left), and Giselle, 2nd act (right). Ballet by V. de Saint Georges and T. Gautier, music by A. Adam, choreography by J. Coralli. Revival, presented by Vic-Wells Ballet, Sadler's Wells Theatre, London.

Icare and Beach

P. M. Larthe. Costumes for " Icare "—Icare (left), Dedale (right). Ballet by Serge Lifar, rhythms by S. Lifar, orchestrated by J. E. Szyfer, choreography by Serge Lifar. Presented at Opéra, Paris, 1935. (Courtesy of the Musée de l'Opéra.)

Photo : A. J. Vaughan, London

Scene from " Beach." Setting and costumes by Raoul Dufy. Ballet by R. Kerdyk, music by Jean Françaix, choreography by Leonide Massine. Presented by Ballets Russes de Monte Carlo, Théâtre de Monte Carlo, 1933.

Scene from "Mozartiana." Costumes and designs by Christian Bérard. Ballet with music by Mozart, choreography by George Balanchine. Revival, as presented by American Ballet Co., New York, 1936.

André Derain. Costumes for "Dreams." Ballet by A. Derain, music by George Antheil, choreography by George Balanchine. Revival, as presented by American Ballet Co., New York, 1935.

Casse Noisette and The Nursery Suite

Photo : Raoul Barba, Monte Carlo

Scene from " Casse Noisette," Act I, Scene II. Ballet with music by P. I. Tchaikovsky. Revival, with choreography by Boris Romanov, as presented by René Blum's Ballets de Monte Carlo, Alhambra Theatre, London, 1936.

Photo : J. W. Debenham, London

Scene from " The Nursery Suite." Setting by William Chappell. Ballet with music by Sir Edward Elgar, choreography by Ninette de Valois. Presented by Vic-Wells Ballet, Sadler's Wells Theatre, London.

Mitislav Dobuzhinsky. Setting for "Les Sylphides." Ballet to music by Chopin, choreography by Michel Fokine. Revival, as presented by Lithuanian Ballet, Alhambra Theatre, London, 1935.

Mitislav Dobuzhinsky. Setting for "The Dwarf Grenadier." Ballet with music by H. Preston, choreography by Nicholas Zverev. Presented by Lithuanian Ballet, Alhambra Theatre, London, 1935.

Pocahontas and Harlequin for President

Scene from "Pocahontas." Costumes by Theodore de Bry. Ballet with music by Elliott Carter, choreography by Lew Christensen. Presented by The Ballet Caravan, New York, 1936.

Scene from "Harlequin for President." Costumes by Keith Martin. Ballet to music by Scarlatti, choreography by Eugene Loring. Presented by The Ballet Caravan, New York, 1936.

Guzstav Oláh. Costumes for "Kuruc Fairy Tale." Ballet by Zsolt Harsányi, music by Zoltán Kodály, choreography by Aurel Millos and Rezsö Brada. Presented by the Royal Hungarian State Ballet, Royal Opera House, Budapest, 1935.

Costumes by Phyllis Dolton

Phyllis Dolton. Costume for "Espagnol" (Dance composed by Anton Dolin). Costume for Ballet—1815 period.

Phyllis Dolton. Costume for "The Nightingale and the Rose"—The Young Girl. Costume for a grotesque Chinese Dance.

Le Pavillon

Cecil Beaton. Setting and costumes for "Le Pavillon." Ballet with music by Borodine, choreography by David Lichine. Presented by Col. W. de Basil's Ballets Russes, Royal Opera House, Covent Garden, London, 1936.

Hugh Stevenson. Back-cloth and two costume designs for "Le Jardin aux Lilas." Ballet by Antony Tudor, music by Chausson, choreography by Antony Tudor. Presented by Ballet Rambert, Mercury Theatre, London, 1936.

Scene from "Coppelia," Act II. Settings and costumes designed by Mitislav Dobuzhinsky, book by Nuitter and Saint-Léon, music by L. Delibes, choreography by Nicholas Zverev. Revival, as presented by René Blum's Ballets de Monte Carlo, Alhambra Theatre, London, 1936.

Photos: Raoul Barba, Monte Carlo

Scene from "Aubade." Settings and costumes by A. Cassandre, music by F. Poulenc, choreography by George Balanchine. Revival, as presented by René Blum's Ballets de Monte Carlo, Alhambra Theatre, London, 1936.

Cecil Beaton. Two settings for "Apparitions"—Prologue and Scene I. Ballet arranged by Constant Lambert to music of Liszt, choreography by Frederick Ashton. Presented by Vic-Wells Ballet, Sadler's Wells Theatre, London, 1936.

David Triomphant

Fernand Léger. Two settings for "David Triomphant," Scenes I and II. Ballet to music by Debussy and Mussorgsky, and rhythms by Serge Lifar, orchestrated by V. Rieti, choreography by Serge Lifar. Presented at Théâtre de la Maison Internationale des Etudiants, Paris, 1936.

Bernard Meninsky. Back-cloth for "David." Ballet by P. Vanda, music by Maurice Jacobson, choreography by Keith Lester. Presented by Markova-Dolin Ballet, Duke of York's Theatre, London, 1936.

Bernard Meninsky. Back-cloth for "Death in Adagio." Ballet by Keith Lester, music by Scarlatti, choreography by Keith Lester. Presented by Markova-Dolin Ballet, King's Theatre, Southsea, England, 1936.

Big City and *Sailors' Love*

Hein Heckroth. Costumes for "Impressions of a Big City." Ballet by Kurt Jooss, music by Alexander Tansman, choreography by Kurt Jooss. Presented by Ballets Jooss, Opera House, Cologne, 1932.

Hein Heckroth. Setting for "Sailors' Love." Ballet and choreography by Sigurd Leeder. Presented by Ballets Jooss, 1936.

Pavel Tchelitchev. Setting for "Orpheus." Opera-ballet by Gluck, choreography by George Balanchine. Presented by American Ballet Co., New York, 1936.

Pavel Tchelitchev : Costume for a Fury in "Orpheus," Act II.

Le Baiser de la Fee and Valentine's Eve

Sophie Fedorovich. (Left) Costume for "Le Baiser de la Fée"—The Fairy. Ballet with music by I. Stravinsky, choreography by Frederick Ashton. Presented by Vic-Wells Ballet, Sadler's Wells Theatre, London, 1936. (Right) Costume for "Valentine's Eve" (see below.)

Sophie Fedorovich. Setting for "Valentine's Eve." Ballet with music by Ravel, choreography by Frederick Ashton. Presented by Ballet Rambert, Duke of York's Theatre, London, 1935.

L'Epreuve d'Amour

Photo : Raoul Barba, Monte Carlo

Scene from "L'Epreuve d'Amour." Setting and Costumes by André Derain. Ballet by A. Derain and M. Fokine, music by Mozart, choreography by Michel Fokine. Presented by René Blum's Ballets de Monte Carlo, Théâtre de Monte Carlo, 1936.

The Love of the Three Pomegranates

Two scenes (VIII and III) from "The Love of the Three Pomegranates." Setting by Nicholas Benois. Ballet with music by G. C. Sonzogno, choreography by Michel Fokine. Presented at Scala Theatre, Milan, 1936.

Photos: Crimella, Milan

Scene from " Csárdajelenet " (Inn Scene). Setting and costumes designed by Zoltan Fülöp. Ballet by Viktor Lányi, music by Jenö Hubay, choreography by Gyula Harangozó. Presented by Royal Hungarian State Ballet, Royal Opera House, Budapest, 1936.

Photos: Vajda M. Pal, Budapest

Scene from "Szent Fáklya" (The Holy Torch). Setting and costumes by Zoltan Fülöp. Ballet by Elsa von Galafres, music by Ernst von Dohnányi, choreography by Elsa von Galafres and Rezsö Brada. Presented by Royal Hungarian State Ballet, Royal Opera House, Budapest, 1934.

Casse-Noisette

Mitislav Dobuzhinsky. Setting and costumes for "Casse-Noisette," Act II. Revival, as presented by Vic-Wells Ballet, Sadler's Wells Theatre, London, 1936.

Photo : Raoul Barba, Monte Carlo

Scene from "Les Sylphides." Based on painting by Corot. Ballet to music by Chopin, choreography by Michel Fokine. Revival, as presented by René Blum's Ballets de Monte Carlo, Alhambra Theatre, London, 1936.

Scene from "The Birds." Setting by M. Zampini. Ballet with music by O. Respighi, choreography by Margarete Wallmann. Presented at Scala Theatre, Milan, 1937.

Lost Illusions

V. V. Dmitriev. Two settings for "Lost Illusions." Ballet based on Balzac's "Illusions Perdues," with music by Asafiev. Presented by Soviet State Ballet.

I. Rabinovich. Two scene models for "La Belle au Bois Dormant." Ballet by Marius Petipa, music by Tchaikovsky, choreography by Marius Petipa. Revival, as presented by the Soviet State Ballet.

The Rake's Progress

Rex Whistler. Setting for Scene I, and Act-drop for "The Rake's Progress." The wings form a permanent setting, the back-cloth being changed according to the exigencies of each scene. It is of interest to compare this setting with that of Claud Lovat Fraser for "The Beggar's Opera." Ballet with music by Gavin Gordon, choreography by Ninette de Valois. Presented by Vic-Wells Ballet, Sadler's Wells Theatre, London, 1935.

Photos: J. W. Debenham, London

La Boutique Fantasque and *Concurrence*

Scene from "La Boutique Fantasque." Setting and costumes by André Derain. Ballet to music by Rossini, choreography by Leonide Massine. Revival, as presented by Col. W. de Basil's Ballets Russes, 1936.

Photos : Raoul Barba, Monte Carlo

Scene from "La Concurrence." Setting and costumes by André Derain. Ballet with music by Georges Auric, choreography by George Balanchine. Presented by Les Ballets Russes de Monte Carlo, Théâtre de Monte Carlo, 1932.

Jota Aragonesa

Mariano Andreù. Setting and costumes for "Jota Aragonesa." Ballet to music by Glinka, choreography by Michel Fokine. Revival, as presented by René Blum's Ballets de Monte Carlo, Coliseum Theatre, London, 1937.

Scene from "Symphonie Fantastique," Vision III. Settings and costumes designed by Christian Bérard. Ballet to music by Berlioz, choreography by Leonide Massine. Presented by Col. W. de Basil's Ballets Russes, Royal Opera House, Covent Garden, London, 1936.

Don Juan

Scene from "Don Juan." Proscenium and curtain designed by Mariano Andreù. Ballet by Eric Allatini and Michel Fokine, music by Gluck, choreography by Michel Fokine. Presented by René Blum's Ballets de Monte Carlo, Alhambra Theatre, London, 1936. Dances and mimed scenes are given in front of the curtain, which is drawn aside to reveal the main scene.

Mariano Andreù. Costumes for "Don Juan." Ballet, by Eric Allatini and Michel Fokine, to music by Gluck, choreography by Michel Fokine. Presented by René Blum's Ballets de Monte Carlo, Alhambra Theatre, London, 1936.

Irene Sharaff : Costume for "The Card Party" —The Queen of Diamonds.

Below :
Scene from "The Card Party"—The Four Queens and Joker. Costumes by Irene Sharaff. Ballet by I. Stravinsky and Maliev ; music by Igor Stravinsky ; choreography by George Balanchine. Presented by American Ballet Co., Metropolitan Opera House, New York, 1937.

Photos : Maharadze, New York

Scenes from "Lumawig," Act II, and, below, Act I. Settings and costumes by Prince Mario Cito Filomarino. Ballet by M. Lualdi, music by A. Lualdi, choreography by Boris Romanov. Presented at Royal Opera, Rome, 1937.

Photos : Comm. Reale, Rome

Hugh Stevenson. Setting for "Le Lac des Cygnes," Act II, and, below, two costumes—Odette, Act II (left), and Prince Siegfried (right). Ballet by Begitchev and Geltser, music by P. I. Tchaikovsky, choreography by Marius Petipa and L. I. Ivanov. Revival, as presented by the Vic-Wells Ballet, Sadler's Wells Theatre, London, 1937.

La Bien Aimee

George Kirsta. Setting and two costumes for "La Bien Aimée." Ballet by A. Benois, music by Schubert and Liszt, choreography by Bronislava Nijinska. Revival, as presented by the Markova-Dolin Ballet, King's Theatre, Hammersmith, London, 1937.

Le Baiser de la Fee

Scene from " Le Baiser de la Fée." Setting by Alice Halicka. Ballet with music by I. Stravinsky, choreography by George Balanchine. Presented by American Ballet Co., New York, 1937. Below, two costumes by Alice Halicka for the same ballet.

Circus ballet and *Terminal*

Marjorye Ffoulkes-Jones. Curtain for a Circus ballet, 1937.

Angelo Pinto. Setting for "Terminal." Ballet with music by Herbert Kingsley, choreography by Catherine Littlefield. Presented by Philadelphia Ballet Co., Hippodrome, London, 1937.

Costumes by Ruth Page

Photo : Maurice Seymour, Chicago (and below)

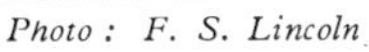

Photo : F. S. Lincoln

Types of costumes used in the Modern Dance as exemplified in the compositions of Ruth Page. (1) Figure in Space. Designed by R. Page and I. Noguchi. (2) Bacchanale. (3) Variations on Euclid. Designed by R. Page and N. Remisov. (4) Promenade. Designed by N. Remisov.

Les Patineurs

William Chappell. Setting and costumes for "Les Patineurs." Ballet to music by Meyerbeer, choreography by Frederick Ashton. Presented by Vic-Wells Ballet, Sadler's Wells Theatre, London, 1937.

Dmitri Bouchenne. Setting and costumes for "Les Elements." Ballet to music by Mozart, choreography by Michel Fokine. Presented by René Blum's Ballets de Monte Carlo, Coliseum Theatre, London, 1937.

Angelo Pinto. Setting for "Barn Dance," and three costumes (The City Slicker, The Light Maiden and The Deacon). Ballet by Catherine Littlefield, music by J. Powell and D. Guion, choreography by Catherine Littlefield. Presented by Philadelphia Ballet Co., Hippodrome, London, 1937.

The Wedding Bouquet

Lord Berners. Setting and two costumes for "The Wedding Bouquet." Ballet with music by Lord Berners, choreography by Frederick Ashton. Presented by Vic-Wells Ballet, Sadler's Wells Theatre, London, 1937.

Nocturne

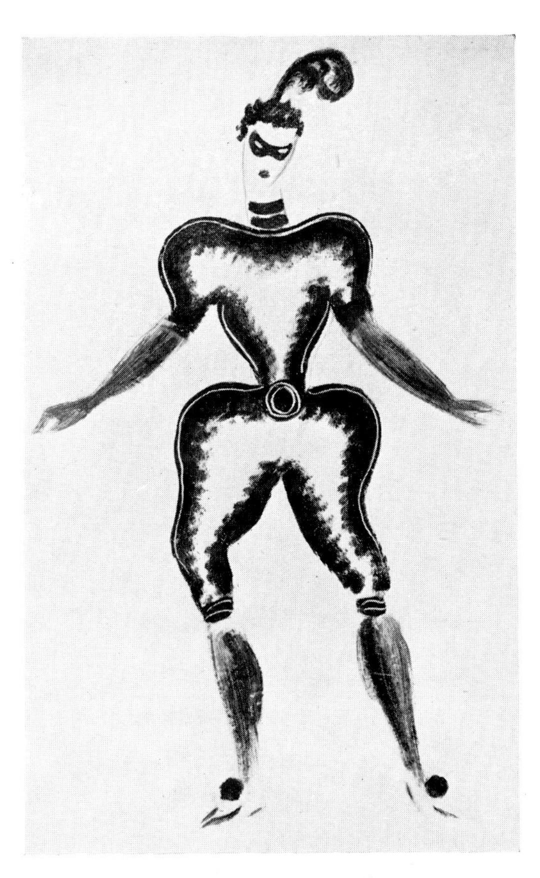

Sophie Fedorovich. Setting and two costumes for " Nocturne." Ballet to music by Delius, choreography by Frederick Ashton. Presented by Vic-Wells Ballet, Sadler's Wells Theatre, London, 1936.

Paul Colin. Setting for "Finances." Ballet presented by Ballets de Paris, 1937.

Paul Colin. Backcloth for "Rugby." Ballet presented at Casino de Paris, Paris, 1931.

Two Hungarian Ballets

Scene from "Csongor és Tünde." Setting and Costumes by Gusztav Oláh. Ballet by L. Márkus, music by L. Weiner, choreography by Jan Cieplinsky. Presented by Royal Hungarian State Ballet, Royal Opera House, Budapest, 1930.

Scene from "Jószi the Wise." Setting by Zoltan Fülöp. Ballet by E. Mohacsi and L. Márkus. music by G. Kósa, choreography by Jan Cieplinsky. Presented by Royal Hungarian State Ballet, Royal Opera House, Budapest, 1933.

Photos: Crimella, Milan

Scene from "Sieba." Setting by Antonio Rovescalli and G .B. Santoni, costumes by Caramba. Ballet by L. Manzotti, music by R. Marenco, choreography by Luigi Manzotti. Revival, as presented at Scala Theatre, Milan, 1935.

Scene from "Old Milan," Scene 6. Setting by Antonio Rovescalli and G. B. Santoni. Ballet by G. Adami, music by F. Vittadini, choreography by Leonide Massine. Presented at Scala Theatre, Milan, 1935.

La Princesse Cygne and *Gallant Assembly*

B. Bilinsky. Setting for "La Princesse Cygne." Ballet with music by Rimsky-Korsakov, choreography by Bronislava Nijinska. Second Version. Presented by Nijinska's Théâtre de la Danse, Paris, 1932.

Hugh Stevenson. Costumes for "Gallant Assembly." Ballet by A. Tudor, to music by Tartini, choreography by Antony Tudor. Presented at Playhouse, Oxford, 1937.

Costumes by Eric Agnew

Eric Agnew. Costume for "Mozart Trio," and for a Faun; the latter is of particular interest for its practical directions to the dressmaker.

La Veuve dans le Miroir and Anna Anna

Photo : Damgaard, Copenhagen

Scene from "La Veuve dans le Miroir." Setting and Costumes by Kjeld Abell, ballet by K. Abell, music by B. Christensen, choreography by Börge Ralov. Presented at Theatre Royal, Copenhagen.

Photo : Mydtskov, Copenhagen

Scene from "Anna Anna, or The Seven Capital Sins." Setting and Costumes by Svend Johannsen, ballet based on Poems by Bert Brecht, music by Kurt Weill, choreography by Harald Lander. Presented at Theatre Royal, Copenhagen.